Golf
IN TEXAS

JOE JAMES

Lone Star Books®
A Division of Gulf Publishing Company
Houston, Texas

T0168396

NOTHIN'S FUNNIER THAN
Golf
IN TEXAS

Gulf Publishing Company
Book Division
P.O. Box 2608 ☐ Houston, Texas 77252-2608

10   9   8   7   6   5   4   3   2   1

Library of Congress Cataloging-in-Publication Data

James, Joe.
    Nothin's funnier than golf in Texas / Joe James.
        p.   cm.
    ISBN 0-88415-294-4 (pbk.)
    1. Golf—Texas—Humor.   I. Title.
GV967.J326   1999
796.352'09764—dc21

98-37662
CIP

Printed on Acid-Free Paper
Printed in the United States of America

Names, situations, and golfers depicted in this book are fictitious. Any resemblance to actual persons or similarity to names of people, living or dead, is coincidental and not intentional.

SPECIAL THANKS

A deep bow of appreciation to Peggy James for her help in editing, proofing and marketing this opus. Also to Mark James for valued counsel and encouragement.

Thanks are also in order to the golfers who daily slug their way past our Texas home and inspire, among other things, this update of James Whitcomb Riley's lines:

> Let me live in a house
> By the side of the course
> In a palace or a hut
> And sketch the funny golfers
> As they try to sink a putt!

OTHER BOOKS
BY THE AUTHOR

Kill It Before It Moves
Quiet On The Tee
What It Is, Is Golf
So You Are Taking Up Golf
How To Give Up Golf
What The Hell Is Trumps?
Teacher Wore A Parachute
100 Funniest Golf Limericks

FOREword

You may have played golf among the dunes of Scotland, the lush hills of Hawaii, or alongside the crashing surf of Pebble Beach. But if you haven't played golf in Texas, pardner, you all ain't really played golf yet!

The next 92 pages highlight the typical Texas golfers, unique animals, and unusual terrains you'll meet if you tackle Texas courses.

And when you tee up your ball to drive, "Drive Friendly." For neither the javelinas or golfers will bite unless provoked.

You all have fun now, you hear!

"When Ah die, Ah'd kinda like to come back to Texas and play golf!"

"Is it too late to press?"

"If I know fire ants he is gonna miss that
putt!"

"Here on the coast you <u>really</u> need to keep your head down!"

"Watch me outrun his drive!"

"This course is rated the toughest in
Texas!"

"Take a drop!   Take a drop!"

"Cheer up!   The next hole is downwind!"

"Down here in Texas the sun gits on you
like ugly on a gorilla!"

"This is the longest par 5 in Texas!"

"Another of those !#*!Titleist birds has laid
an egg in our nest!"

"Don't even <u>think</u> about it!"

"Come on George! This shot could win the
match!"

"Are you sayin' Ah cheat?   Go for youah
putter!"

"Mine is an old ball. How about yours?"

"Shut up! I am putting for a birdie!"

"The geology in Texas is fantastic. Each
hole takes you farther back in time!"

"Gimmie full flaps!"

"Reckon Ah better have my wedge!"

THE TEXAS OPEN

24

"She can't count!   There's only two of us!"

"What are you Yankees starin' at?"

"Here in Texas, Ma'am, rains can come up
kinda sudden!"

"We are much safer near these flags!"

"Ah do not recommend you doin' anything
foolish like countin' strokes!"

"Why don't we just skip this hole!"

A Texas dermatologist plays golf in August.

"Congratulations! You all are the new
Texas Open champion!"

"Our Texas fairways get hard in the
summer.   Use your wedge!"

"I hope you all brought extra balls."

"They are supposed to be smarter than us
but look who is in the shade!"

"Floods like this come every hundred
years -- or every other year!"

"Putt at the fire ants. They'll carry it to the hole!"

"Dammit lady! We told you all to fix your
ball marks on the green!"

"If you got on in two, you could get an
eagle on this hole!"

"I hear you been kinda' off your game!"

"It breaks right, then left, then right--and
from then on it is straight in!"

"Since Bill started to putt, this is the second
time that turtle has crossed the green!"

"Our deer here in Texas are most helpful!"

"We musta' took a wrong turn. We are in
Mexico!"

"If Ah wuz you, Ah wouldn't step back to
line up my putt!"

"Gimmie mah No.3 Winchester!"

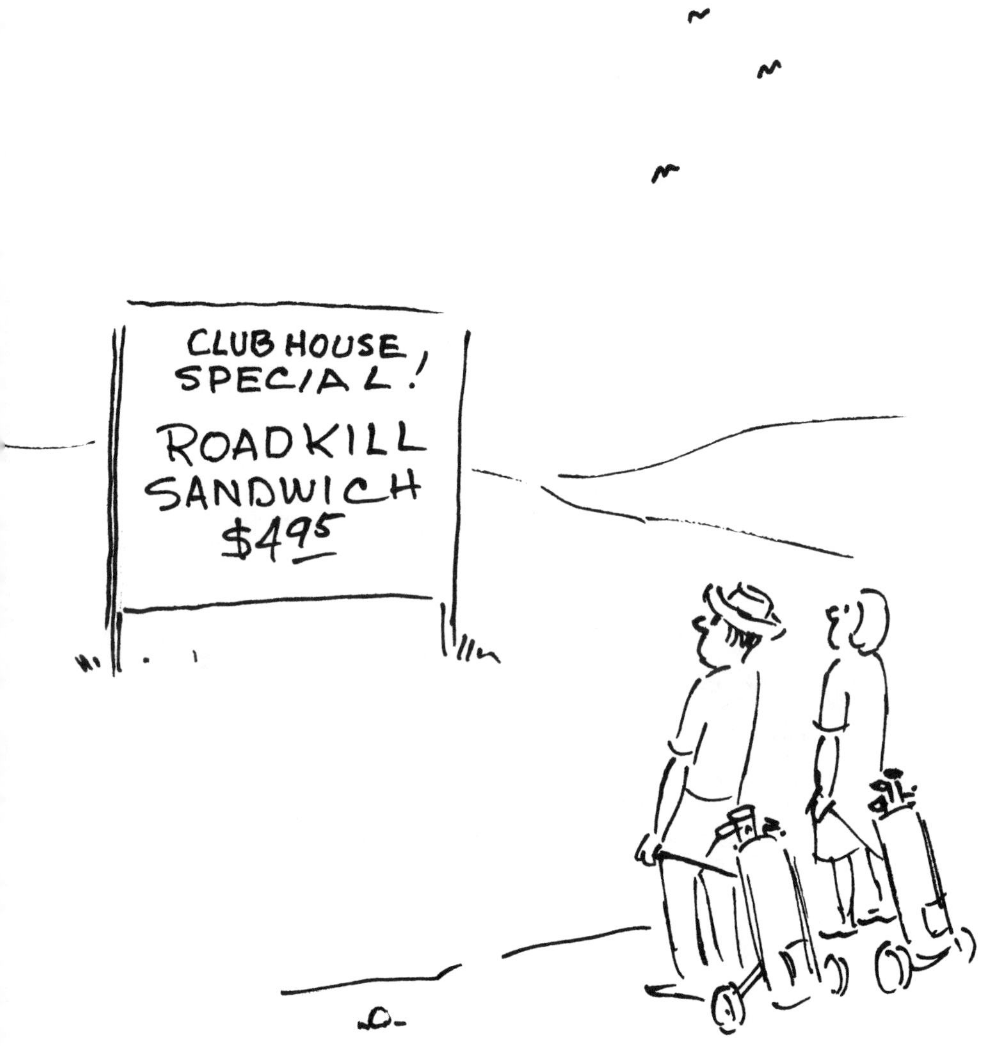
CLUB HOUSE SPECIAL!
ROADKILL SANDWICH $4.95

"Sit on it!   We might hatch a golfer!"

"This is a <u>long</u> par 5. When you reach the
green, set your watch up an hour!"

"Don't eat it! Don't eat it!"

"He is one of the toughest golfers in all of
Texas!"

"Hang around. If he misses that fourth
putt he may end it all!"

"Ah love Texas so much Ah hate
to take a divot!"

"Ah know real Texans play in all kind
of weather- but this hail sure
makes it hard to find your ball!"

"Now down there is where you'll be
glad you are in a shell!"

WHEN TEXANS TAKE UP GOLF

"I've heard of Snow Bird golfers but
you are the first one I've seen!"

"We better get back to the fort!"

"It is times like this when Ah am
especially proud to be a Texan!"

"Don't stop that horny toad! He's
heading for the green!"

"Sure you can get there with a seven iron--
if you hit it often enough!"

"I told you we play golf in Texas
the year 'round!"

"Hope you all don't mind if Ah watch
the Texas-OU football game?"

"Ah believe it will help if you all
stand right behind the hole!""

"You come back here and putt out!"

"Here comes the first bunch of geese
flyin' South. The Winter Texans
won't be far behind!"

"Ah need to stop at the Pro shop and
buy me some new clubs. Ah got mine
dirty on the front nine!"

"Just think! Cabeza de Vaca probably
came right through here!"

"But when Spring comes to Texas
Snowbirds _always_ go home!"

"Ah would love to shoot my age, but
Ah may not live that long!"

"Will you please stop humming
'Beautiful, Beautiful Texas?'"

"Oh look!   There's a Chachalaca!"

"Naturally Ah want golf cleats on 'em!"

"Ah think Schultz cheats--but keep
it under your hat!"

"They have revised the course a little.
The Governor is gonna play here
tomorrow"

"This tree is a pin oak. That one is
a hackberry, and that other one is
a madrone. Texas has 60 varieties!"

"Would you mind telling me where the
sand traps start-- and stop?"

"The noise can bother putting but the
oil sure lubricates our club dues!"

"Youah ball is right where General Sam Houston rested before the Battle of San Jacinto!"

"Any <u>real</u> Texas Gentleman would
give me this putt!"

"Hot damn!   You all done struck oil!"

"If you all are through talkin' about
the game, Ah'd like to say a
few words about Texas!"

"Madam, Ah apologize for mah language.
But apparently you ain't ever
missed no !*!#! three foot putt!"

"That masked man--who mows and goes
and nobody knows--is the Lawn Ranger!"

"This will teach you men not to try
and play golf on Ladies' Day!"

"Luke is a <u>real</u> Texan. He refuses
to play the North course!"

"That ain't as hard as tryin' to sink
a 10-foot sidehill putt!"

"How come you can remember the Alamo
but keep forgetting your strokes?"

"George, you are absolutely right!
We really are what we eat!"

"Thank Goodness! Ah thought that smell
was mah puttin'!"